The
Immigration
Solution

The Immigration Solution

An Amnesty-Free End to Illegal
Immigration in Three Years

By A. C. American

Book Layout © 2014 BookDesignTemplates.com

The Immigration Solution / A. C. American. -- 1st ed.
ISBN 978-0-9967467-0-0

Dedicated to restoring order in America

Contents

Preface

For years we have all witnessed our nation's immigration problems manifesting themselves in many different ways. The situation not only burdens our welfare and education systems, it also puts illegal workers (and many employers) in violation of the law. And it has chained us as a nation to a labor and revenue source that is at its base illegal.

After years of failed policies, most of us are pessimistic about resolving the situation. We have watched our politicians on both sides of the aisle either ignore these problems or make the problems even worse by their action or inaction. For a long time I was right there with you: talking back to the radio, yelling at the TV, and complaining to like-minded friends.

But at some point I got serious and stopped "armchair quarterbacking" the problem. I watched what was going on and I thought more deeply; I researched; then I researched more and I talked with a lot of people. Now I feel compelled to share what

I've found: (1) a clear, factual explanation of how we got here, (2) a nonpartisan description of our current problems, and (3) a simple *Way Forward for America: The Immigration Solution.*

You'll have noticed from the cover that I have a pen name. And of course you want to know who I really am, because we all purchase our books based on the author's expertise as well as the subject matter. But the trouble is, *all* discussion of immigration issues is so politically charged that everyone's vision is immediately distorted by one "side" or the other because of the author's pedigree, supposed motives, politics, marital status—in other words, by the very identity of the author. That is why I am writing this book anonymously.

So who am I? *It doesn't matter.*

There are only a few things you need to know about me: (1) I don't have a voter base to impress, (2) I seek absolutely no notoriety, and (3) I am a nonpartisan author. This text contains no references to either political party and no name calling. No political positions on the spectrum of left to right are taken. I have no interest in identifying, blaming, or demonizing any individual or political group for our current situation.

What I do have are a few ideas about how our immigration problems might be solved. I offer no massive reinvention of anything, no kingdom building, and no need for amnesty—just a reasoned, thoughtful, and workable solution. All that matters to me is that you read this book, research the content, understand the magnitude of the problem, and as a result are inspired to move the program forward and implement the solution.

I see Americans of all ethnicities, genders, and ages, unclear and unsure what to do about the untold millions of people living illegally in their midst. Everyone is looking for a solution for the mass of humanity living in the shadows. Here, in this brief handbook, I believe you will find The Immigration Solution.

I would respectfully request that you set aside your current views and beliefs about our immigration problem and read this book with an open mind. Perhaps you will discover, as I did, that most of what we have been told about the "Immigration Problem" isn't true. Please let me share my journey with you.

But first, just a few words about the terminology I chose to use in this book.

Immigrants, Aliens, or Migrant Workers?

All Americans, even those who are not politically aware, have strong opinions on immigration. This topic has been so politicized that many of us have difficulty discussing it in mixed company. Any discussion of the topic can be quickly derailed if the wrong words are used to describe the immigrants among us.

Some of the confusion regarding illegal immigration is generated by the interchangeable use of these three different terms: "immigrants," "aliens," and "migrant workers." For the sake of discussion, let's look at the Dictionary.com definitions:

> **Immigrant**: "A person who migrates to another country, usually for *permanent residence*" (emphasis mine).

> **Alien**: "1. A resident born in or belonging to another country who has not acquired citizenship by naturalization. 2. A foreigner."

Migrant Worker: "A person who moves from place to place to get work, especially a farm laborer who harvests crops seasonally."

When you add "illegal" or "undocumented" to the front of any of these three labels, the meaning is changed; now *none* of these terms refers to individuals possessing legal authorization to be present in America.

For the sake of discussion, we will define these three terms as follows:

"Illegal immigrants" are noncitizens who have no legal authorization to be in this country but who wish to abandon their country of origin and become U.S. citizens. They are actively engaged in learning to speak the English language and in educating themselves about how our nation is structured so they can pass the Citizenship Test.

"Illegal aliens" are noncitizens with no authorization to be in this country who maintain their allegiance to their home country. (Author's note: Illegal aliens are proud of their national origin; they consider their nation of origin to be *home.*)

"Illegal migrant workers" are noncitizens with no authorization to be in this country who nonetheless want to work here for an unknown period of time (or to fulfill a monetary goal) while sending money home. They intend to return to their country of origin.

For the sake of clarity, I will use "illegal alien" to describe those foreigners who have entered America illegally. I have chosen this term because it most accurately describes their legal status and because this term is used in federal legislation. *My use of this term is in no way meant to be demeaning, derogatory, or disrespectful.*

I use this term because it accurately describes the true nature and character of the individuals in question and their legal status in America.

Summary: The Real Truth

What is an illegal alien?

• An illegal alien is a citizen of another country who is residing in the United States illegally.

$$\oint$$

Chapter 1

The Dilemma

That illegal immigration has been such a large problem for so long in America is mind numbing. No matter how old you are, it has been a reoccurring topic of political conversation all of our lives!

So what's the problem? It is hard to know where to begin. My research has generated an absolute avalanche of information. Much of the information is so colored by political bias that it is unusable. Much of it is written to further reinforce and advance a particular political point of view, not to honestly understand the issues at hand.

It is my goal to strip away the political bias (a.k.a. "the spin") and provide you with the relevant facts you need to make a well-reasoned determination about the *Way Forward for America*.

The History of Illegal Immigration

The United States has been dealing with the issue of illegal immigration since its early days, as a quick summary of the first U.S. legislation on immigration reveals. Legal immigration in American began with:

> ... the original United States Naturalization Law of March 26, 1790, which provided the first rules to be followed by the United States in granting of national citizenship. This law limited naturalization to immigrants who were free, white persons of good character. It thus excluded American Indians, indentured servants, slaves, free blacks, and Asians. It also provided for citizenship for the children of U.S. citizens born abroad, but specified that the right of citizenship did "not descend to persons whose fathers have never been resident in the United States." It specifies that such children shall be considered as natural born citizens.
>
> In order to address one's good character, the law required two years of residence in the United States and one year in the state of residence, prior to applying for citizenship. When those requirements were met, an immigrant could file

a petition for naturalization with any common-law court of record having jurisdiction over his residence. Once convinced of the applicant's good moral character, the court would administer an oath of allegiance to support the Constitution of the United States. The clerk of the court was to make a record of the proceedings, and "thereupon such person shall be considered as a citizen of the United States."[1]

On April 30, 1803, President Thomas Jefferson (1801–1809) completed the purchase of 828,000 miles of land that stretched from the Mississippi River to the Rocky Mountains and from the Gulf of Mexico to Canada. This deal, known as the Louisiana Purchase, nearly doubled the size of the United States. Illegal immigration was not a major concern at this time because America was so vast. The Purchase was the genesis of the nation's westward expansion. By the 1840s, many Americans believed that it was Americas' Manifest Destiny to stretch from coast to coast.

The other events of the day—the discovery of gold in California in 1848, the Gadsden Purchase of

---

1. "Naturalization Act of 1790," Wikipedia website. Available at: www.Wikipedia.org/wiki/Naturalization_Act_of_1790.

1853 (which fixed the boundaries of "the lower 48" where they are today), the building of the Trans-continental Railroad (1863–1869), etc.—fueled the westward settlement of America. Concerns about immigration, both legal and illegal, became almost nonexistent.

Illegal immigration did not become a problem until the late nineteenth century. The first general federal Immigration Act was approved in 1882 under the presidential administration of Chester A. Arthur (1881–1885). "Arthur approved a measure that excluded paupers, criminals, and lunatics. Congress suspended Chinese immigration for 10 years, later making the restriction permanent."[2] While this legislation affected only a small number of people, it made the lawful distinction between legal and illegal immigration. Before this, migration (immigration) was barely regulated.

In 1892, 10 years after the passage of the Immigration Act of 1882 and the Chinese Exclusion Act (also in 1882), Ellis Island opened as a federal immigration station. It served that purpose for more than 60 years, closing in 1954. During the large

2. "Chester A. Arthur," The White House website. Available at: www.whitehouse.gov /1600/presidents/chesterarthur.

wave of immigration from 1881 to 1920, nearly 23.5 million immigrants poured into the United States.

After World War I, "President Warren G. Harding (1921–1923) sign[ed] the Immigration Quota Act into law in 1921, after booming postwar immigration resulted in 500,971 people passing through Ellis Island. According to the new law, annual immigration from any country cannot exceed 3% of the total number of immigrants from a country living in the U.S. (according to Census data) in 1920. The National Origins Act of 1924 goes even further, limiting total annual immigration to 165,000 and fixing quotas of immigrants from specific countries."[3]

Starting with the stock market crash in 1929, the United States further tightened visa rules. As the jobs dried up, many illegal aliens returned home. "By 1932, the Great Depression had taken hold in the U.S., and for the first time more immigrants left the country than arrived."[4] It is estimated that between 1929 and 1939, 500,000 to 1 million Mexicans left the United States.

---

3. "Ellis Island," History.com website. Available at: www.history.com/topics/ellis-island.

4. Ibid.

The exodus of Mexican nationals continued during the Herbert Hoover administration (1929–1933). The policy of repatriation reached its peak at the end of that administration. This policy applied to all alien groups, not just Mexicans. Hoover and many others believed that the aliens were taking jobs from Americans. For these and other reasons he actively supported the effort to reduce legal and illegal entries into the country. Even then, in February 1928, there were hearings in the Senate about the burden of the unrestricted flow of Mexican nationals on the state's taxpayers, prisons, hospitals, schools, and on American workers' wages.

During Franklin Roosevelt's administration (1933–1945) deportation and repatriations declined. The only notable exception was in July 1935, when Roosevelt ordered a large deportation of alien criminals but exempted Mexican and Canadian detainees. The concern was that if they were deported to their country of origin they could easily return.

Illegal immigration really got its start in the war years, the 1940s. Labor shortages due to the war effort caused the federal government to set up a program to import Mexican laborers to work temporarily in agriculture, primarily in the Southwest.

This was called the Bracero Program. The program was structured to temporarily import migrant workers to harvest crops. Once the harvest was completed they were to return home.

Originally Braceros were supposed to be hired only if the number of Americans found to harvest the crop was inadequate. For the Braceros, this was their first opportunity to escape their impoverished existence in Mexico. Understandably, many did not want to return to that poverty. Over the next 20 years, 5 million Mexican workers discovered that for the same hard work that they had done in Mexico they could earn a much better living in America. Indeed, most of the South American countries have no significant social safety net. In pursuit of a better life, these aliens have made themselves indispensable to their American employers. Many still live an austere lifestyle in the United States and send money home to parents and family. Mexico and other South American countries receive over $30 billion annually in transfer payments originating from this country.[5]

---

5. "Remittances on the Rise," May 28, 2015, Geo-Mexico website. Available at: www.geo-mexico.com/?tag=remittances.

The Bracero Program continued to be a flourishing source of cheap labor for U.S. employers in the Southwest. As a result, the number of Mexicans crossing the border grew to about 1 million a year during President Eisenhower's first term (1953–1956). Newspapers, magazines, television news programs, trade publications, and politicians of that time expressed public concern about the devastating impact on American workers' wages caused by the flood of Mexican nationals into the United States. The president took decisive action. He instructed the Immigration and Naturalization Service to launch Operation Wetback. With presidential appointee General Joseph Swing at its head and through the efforts of 1,075 border patrol agents, tens of thousands of illegal aliens were caught and deported back to Mexico. Hundreds of thousands of illegal aliens read the handwriting on the wall and self-deported. By the end of the 1950s, illegal immigration had dropped by 95%. The Bracero Program finally ended in 1964. It succumbed to chronic complaints from unions, citizens, and not surprisingly, Mexican-Americans that these foreigners were taking their jobs.

After the passage of the 1965 Immigration Act, legal immigration increased sharply. Unfortunately, illegal immigration increased as well: The Immigration and Nationality Act of 1965 (a.k.a. the Hart Cellar Act) changed the National Origins Formula that had been in place in the United States since the Emergency Quota Act of 1921. The Hart Cellar Act was proposed by Rep. Emanuel Cellar of New York, cosponsored by Sen. Philip Hart of Michigan, and promoted by Sen. Ted Kennedy of Massachusetts.

> The Hart-Cellar Act abolished the National Origins Quota system that had been American immigration policy since the 1920s, replacing it with a preference system that focused on immigrants' skill and family relationships with citizens or U.S. residents. ...

> In order to convince the American people of the legislation's merits, its proponents assured that [its] passage would not influence America's culture significantly. President Johnson (1963–1969) called the bill "not a revolutionary bill. It does not affect the lives of millions," while Secretary of State Dean Rusk and other politicians, including Sen. Ted Kennedy, hastened to reas-

sure the populace that the demographic mix would not be affected; these assertions would later prove grossly inaccurate.[6]

As with so much federal legislation, "adjustments" needed to be made.

"Since that Immigration and Nationality Act of 1965, Congress has passed seven amnesties:

1. Immigration and Reform Control Act (IRCA), 1986: A blanket amnesty for over 2.7 million illegal aliens

2. Section 245(i) Amnesty, 1994: A temporary rolling amnesty for 578,000 illegal aliens

3. Section 245(i), Extension Amnesty, 1997: An extension of the rolling amnesty created in 1994

4. Nicaraguan Adjustment and Central American Relief Act (NACARA) Amnesty, 1997: An amnesty for close to 1 million illegal aliens from Central America

---

6. "Immigration and Nationality Act of 1965," Wikipedia website. Available at: www.wikipedia.com/wiki/Immigration_and_Nationality_Act_of_1965.

5. Haitian Refugee Immigration Fairness Act (HRIFA) Amnesty, 1998: An amnesty for 125,000 illegal aliens from Haiti

6. Late amnesty, 2000: An amnesty for some illegal aliens who claim they should have been amnestied under the 1986 IRCA amnesty, an estimated 4,000 aliens

7. LIFE Act Amnesty, 2000: A restatement of the rolling Section 245 (i) amnesty, an estimated 900,000 illegal aliens"[7]

The 1986 Immigration Reform and Control Act (IRCA) attempted to limit illegal immigration through:

1. Improving border security,

2. Increased prosecution of employers who hired illegal aliens, and

3. Granting temporary legal status to illegal immigrants who had resided in the country for

---

7. "The Seven Amnesties Passed by Congress," Numbers USA website. Available at: www.numbersusa.com/content/learn/illegal-immigration/seven-amnesties-passed-congress.html.

more than five years and met some certain other conditions. With time, the temporary legal status could be upgraded to citizenship.

President Ronald Reagan (1981–1989) approved this path to citizenship (IRCA, 1986), not fully understanding that it was granting amnesty to almost 3 million people. Widespread document fraud skewed (and hid) the numbers of anticipated beneficiaries.

The Illegal Immigration Reform and Immigration Responsibility Act was passed in 1996, during President Bill Clinton's (1993–2001) administration. Many heads of state from the Caribbean and Central America relied heavily on remittances sent back to their countries from the United States. They were worried that the Clinton Administration might support mass deportation. They lobbied (some for humanitarian reasons) that those income streams not be damaged by mass deportations. Publicly the president supported the IRCA legislation. Despite that support, mass deportations did not materialize. There were about 7 million illegal aliens residing in the United States when he left office.

During the administration of President George W. Bush (2001–2009) illegal immigration continued to grow. There was a measurable and dramatic reduction in enforcement. President Bush actively promoted amnesty, most notably as a supporter of the Comprehensive Immigration Reform Act of 2007. Despite his support, the act was defeated by widespread bipartisan opposition.

So Where Does This Leave Us?

I assume that if you're reading this book, you are at least somewhat politically conscious and are reasonably aware of the state of immigration under the current administration. After all, you are living it!

Our current immigration system is in shambles and it has been further compounded by recent presidential executive orders. The rules, categories / subcategories of special groups, quotas within the immigration bureaucracy, and so on have created a flourishing legal industry. Only lawyers can speak the language of immigration. Ordinary citizens need not apply.

It hasn't helped that on the one hand, the United States seems to invite Mexican immigrants, while on the other hand it pushes them away. Similarly, many Americans are ambivalent toward illegal aliens. They display popular outrage over illegal immigration but show little hostility to individual illegal aliens. Most Americans believe that if they were in the aliens' shoes, they would also be crossing the border to achieve a better life for themselves and their families. This helps explain why in a 2013 Pew Research Center for the People and the Press Poll, "seven in ten Americans (71%) say there should be a way for people in the United States illegally to remain in this country, (if they meet certain requirements), while 27% say they should not be allowed to stay legally."[8]

Americans cease being ambivalent about illegal immigration when amnesty is brought into the conversation: in poll after poll Americans overwhelmingly believe that citizenship should not be awarded to individuals who have entered this country illegally. The website of the Federation for American Immigration Reform (www.fairus.org) contains a summary of illegal immigration and am-

---

8. "Most Say Illegal Immigrants Should Be Allowed to Stay, But Citizenship Is More Divisive," March 28, 2013, Pew Research Center website. Available at: www.people-press.org/2013/03/28/most-say-illegal-immigrants-should-be-allowed-to-stay-but-citizenship-is-more-divisive/.

nesty polls conducted by the following organizations:

- Gallup
- CBS News
- Pew Hispanic Center
- ABC News
- Washington Post
- Rasmussen
- Fox News
- CIS/Pulse
- Reuters
- Wall Street Journal
- NBC News
- FAIR/Pulse
- Quinnipiac
- NY Times
- CNN/Opinion Research
- Zogby[9]

---

9. "Public Opinion Polls on Immigration," FAIR website. Available at: www.fairus.org/facts/public-opinion.

Most Americans, both young and old, are con-
cerned about the long-term viability of Social
Security and Medicare retirement benefits. Award-
ing citizenship to 11 million-plus illegal immigrants
would push our Social Security / Medicare safety
net into insolvency. Americans fundamentally understand that this would destroy America as we
know it.

(For those who are curious, Social Security is
scheduled to deplete the combined trust fund reserves in 2033. The reserve depletion of Medicare is
projected for 2030.[10])

Further, it appears that for many illegal aliens,
particularly those from Mexico, citizenship is not
particularly important. Study after study indicates
that undocumented aliens are not here to stay (immigrate), they are here to earn a living.[11]

Nearly two-thirds of the 5.4 million legal immigrants from Mexico who were eligible to become
U.S. citizens have not yet taken that step. Their rate
of naturalization (36%) is only half that of legal

10. "A Summary of the 2014 Annual Reports," pages 1–5, Social Security website. Available at: www.ssa.gov/oact/trsum/.

11. Anna Gonzales-Barbara, Mark Hugo Lopez, and Jeffrey S. Passel, "The
Path Not Taken," Pew Research Center, Hispanic Trends website, Feb. 4, 2013.
Available at: www.pewhispanic.org/2013/02/04/the-path-not-taken.

immigrants from all other countries combined, according to an analysis of Census Bureau data by the Pew Hispanic Center, a Project of Pew Research. The last time the United States government created a pathway to citizenship for immigrants in the country illegally was in 1986 with the passage of IRCA. "A 2010 study by the U.S. Department of Homeland Security found that 40% of the 2.7 million immigrants who obtained a green card derived from the IRCA had naturalized by 2009."[12]

So for the 11 million-plus illegal aliens already residing in the United States, how important *is* citizenship? Most illegal aliens do not see living in America as a permanent condition. This is why so few illegal aliens purchase homes or learn English. Why bother if they are not going to be here long enough for that skill to be useful? Even those who can establish legal residency for citizenship don't bother as they are not planning to live here permanently. Most plan to earn as much money as they can now and return to their country of origin at a later date.

"By 55% to 35%, Hispanics say that they think being able to live and work in the United States le-

---

12. Ibid.

gally without the threat of deportation is more important for unauthorized immigrants than a pathway to citizenship."[13] These percentages are surprising when you consider the potential economic benefits that the individuals would be able to access as citizens: food stamps, welfare, and any other of the hundreds of federal, state, and local assistance programs. Could it be that illegal aliens are not interested in citizenship because they don't plan to stay long enough to use these benefits?

In Summary

This brief history of immigration is most instructive. It looks like we have done and tried everything before. Like Yogi Berra said: "It's déjà vu all over again."

Here's what we've discovered:

• For most Americans, amnesty, in any form, is off the table.

---

13. Mark Hugo Lopez, Paul Taylor, Cary Funk, and Anna Gonzales-Barbera, "On Immigration Policy, Deportation Relief Seen as More Important than Citizenship," Dec. 9, 2013, Pew Research Center, Hispanic Trends website, www.pewhispanic.org/2013/12/19/on-immigration-policy-deportation-relief-seen-as-more-important-than-citizenship/.

• By and large illegal aliens are here to earn money now and plan to return home later.

• For most illegal aliens, deportation relief is more important than citizenship. It protects their ability to do what they came here for: to earn a living.

In chapter 2 we will examine the exaggerations, untruths, and myths that keep us from achieving an accurate understanding of who the illegal aliens are.

$$\oint$$

Chapter 2

Who Are the Illegal Aliens?

The controversy over illegal migration has affected our politics and policies for decades, causing the public's view of illegal aliens to run the spectrum of political belief, from the extreme left to the extreme right.

Some characterize illegal aliens as harassed by law enforcement, exploited by unscrupulous employers, taken advantage of by mercenary landlords, and even victimized by other illegal aliens. Others characterize illegal aliens as sinister individuals who access public services and government programs to which they are not entitled. They are viewed by many in society as preying on law-abiding Americans by "stealing jobs," participating in "illicit activities," and working "under the table" and thus not paying taxes.

These exaggerations, untruths, and outright myths are roadblocks to any meaningful conversation about immigration reform. These characterizations are profoundly misleading because they are generally presented in the context of a particular political group's agenda. We are living in a partisan, sound bite–driven news cycle where genuine provable facts are rarely part of the conversation. And though we live in the Information Age, where the facts are just a click away on the Internet, many Americans remain oblivious to the truth.

In order to move the immigration discussion forward, we need to discard these distortions and determine in a factual, nonpartisan, and thoughtful way just who the illegal aliens truly are. By carefully researching and seeking out generally accepted, mainstream public sources, one can actually achieve a reasonably accurate understanding of the makeup of the illegal alien population in America. Let's take some of the misperceptions and research them to see what the truth really is.

One source of reliable information is the Pew Research Center and the Pew Research Center's Hispanic Trends Project. These sources estimate that there are more than 11 million undocumented immigrants in the United States, including more than 1 million children under the age of 18.

Another source further refines this information: "As of 2012, the population of immigrants in the United States illegally is estimated to be approximately 11.43 million, roughly 3.7% of the entire U.S. population. 59% of the immigrants in the country illegally are from Mexico, and 25% of all immigrants in the country illegally reside in California."[14] Central America contributes an additional 15% to the illegal alien population.

What Does the Government Know, and When Did They Learn It?

Our first question is, how do illegal aliens get here? The stereotypical image of the way illegal aliens enter the United States is that they sneak across the border one by one, or in small groups. The truth of the matter is that 40% of the 11-plus million un-

---

14. "Demographics of Immigrants in the United States Illegally," updated August 2014, ProCon website. Available at:
www.procon.org/view.resource.php?resourceID=000845.

documented workers entered America *legally* on visitor, work, or student visas.[15]

These people secured legal permission and government approval to enter the United States by producing one of the mandatory documents needed to secure a visa: a passport issued by their country of origin. Because applicants for visitor, work, or student visas are visiting the United States temporarily, they are required to file a statement of nonimmigrant intent, in which they testify and agree in writing to exit the United States on or before the expiration of their visa. But, alas, many have overstayed this date.

In 2011, the Pew Research Hispanic Trends Project estimated that more than three-fifths of adult illegal aliens have been living in the United States for at least 10 years (see Figure 1). More than a fifth had lived here between five and nine years. And only 15% had been here less than five years.[16] Is it really possible that 85% of our illegal

---

15. See Sara Murray, "Many in US Illegally Overstayed Their Visas," Wall Street Journal, April 7, 2013; Data sources: Robert Warren, former director of statistics at the Immigration and Naturalization Service; John Robert Warren, Minnesota Population Center.

16. Paul Taylor, et al., "Unauthorized Immigrants: Length of Residency, Patterns of Parenthood," Pew Research Hispanic Trends Project, December 1, 2011.

Unauthorized Adults by Duration of Residence in U.S., 2010

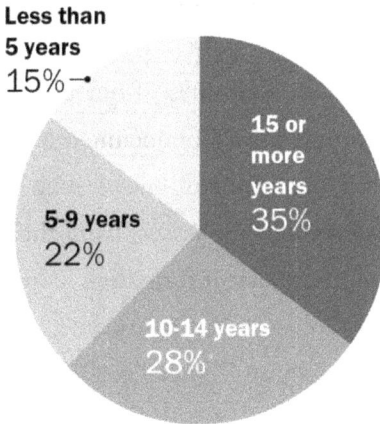

Note: Based on adults ages 18 and older at the time of the survey.

Source: Pew Hispanic Center tabulations of augmented March 2010 Current Population Survey; data adjusted for survey ommissions

PEW RESEARCH CENTER

Figure 1. Reprinted with permission from "Unauthorized Immigrants: Length of Residency, Patterns of Parenthood," Pew Research Center, Washington, DC (December 2011). http://www.pewhispanic.org/2011/12/01/unauthorized-adults-length-of-residency-patterns.

Available at: www.pewhispanic.org/2011/12/01/unauthorized-immigrants-length-of-residency-patterns-of-parenthood/.

alien population has been here for more than 5 years?

These estimates could be easily validated by reviewing IRS taxpayer W-2 information. (Maybe the government doesn't want to publically acknowledge this truth?)

Does this mean that 40% of our undocumented alien population is in reality documented? Is it possible that the government knows who they are? That the government possesses, from their visa applications, all their basic information: copies of their passports, pictures, DOB, fingerprints, assigned tax ID number, and so on? Where is all that documentation today?

What ELSE Does the Government Know, and When Did They Learn THAT!?

The Social Security Administration estimates that 75% of illegal aliens are actually on formal payrolls and are paid by check, just like everyone else. Their employers automatically withhold federal, state, and local income taxes, Social Security, and Medicare taxes.

At the completion of each calendar year every employer must report to federal and state tax entities all wages paid and taxes withheld for every employee on the required Department of the Treasury IRS W-2 Wage and Tax Statement. (If you have further interest, go to www.irs.gov and search for Form W-2).

This W-2 form identifies the employer by Employer Identification Number (EIN) along with complete name and address information. The employee is also identified by Social Security number, and complete name and address information is included as well. The form identifies all wages and taxes paid by the employee and employer to federal and state entities. Electronic copies of this document are transmitted to all government taxing authorities. A triplicate paper copy is mailed to the taxpayer's address of record listed on their W-2 as required by law, to assist in the proper filing of their personal income tax return.

So while it may be fair to say we have 11-plus million undocumented aliens residing in America, it is *not* accurate for us to say that we don't know who and where they are. All taxes paid by employers and employees are electronically reported to state tax authorities on a pay-period-by-pay-period basis. Federal tax authorities receive the data quarterly. This data trail provides all the information needed to determine who and where a particular taxpayer is employed. According to Social Security data, 75% of undocumented aliens are taxpayers. And the government knows just about everything there is to know about them, just like any other taxpayer. The federal government has been collecting W-2 and other related information on these taxpayers for years, just as it has on every legal American taxpayer. So how can they honestly be categorized as "undocumented" aliens?

Just how much money are illegal aliens contributing to Social Security, Medicare, income taxes, property taxes, sales taxes, DMV registration fees, and the like? Here's one explanation, from an article in the *Seattle Times* by John Lantigua:

> Social Security officials keep a record of any wages that do not match up with real names and numbers in their system. The record is called the "earnings suspense file." In 2009, the latest year for which figures are available, employers reported wages of $72.8 billion for 7.7 million workers who could not be matched to legal So-

cial Security numbers. That total [SSA earnings suspense file totals] hit a record of $90.4 billion, earned by 10.8 million workers, in 2007, just before the recession. Some of those were legal workers who simply made paperwork mistakes, but the majority are believed to be illegal aliens.[17]

The SSA notifies employers regarding mismatched names and Social Security numbers. They request, in writing, that the employer double check and resubmit the Social Security numbers that the employee(s) in question provided the employer. Clearly, after several years of this repeated drill, the Social Security Administration must recognize that these named individuals are illegally using another individual's SSN, are breaking the law, and are perhaps even illegal aliens.

Lantigua continues:

Because those wages were reported by employers and not paid under the table, Social Security and Medicare deductions had to be made. A to-

---

17. John Lantigua, "Illegal Immigrants Pay Social Security Benefits," *Seattle Times*, December 8, 2011. Available at: www.seattletimes.com/nation-world/illegal-immigrants-pay-social-secutiry-tax-wont-benefit/.

tal of 12.4 percent of those wages went to the Social Security Administration system (6.2 percent paid by both the worker and the employer). An additional 2.9 percent was paid to Medicare, half by the worker and half by the employer.

That means about $11.2 billion from the wages of illegal aliens went into the Social Security Trust Fund in 2007, and $2.6 billion went into Medicare. While that money will be used to pay retirees and health-care beneficiaries, it will most likely never be claimed by the illegal immigrants who contributed it.[18]

Benefits vs. Aliens

Read the last sentence of the previous paragraph again. "While that money [$14 *billion* for 2007] will be used to pay retirees and health-care beneficiaries [i.e., current liabilities], *it will most likely NEVER be claimed by the illegal immigrants who contributed it." NEVER!!*

Noncitizens (foreigners) are prohibited from receiving federal Social Security Administration and

---

18. Ibid.

Medicare benefits. (However, green card holders and *legal* aliens get Social Security benefits when they retire, if they worked for at least 10 years [40 quarters] before retiring.)

Are our legislators fundamentally unable to reform (enforce) immigration policy because they see the illegal alien as a *cash cow funding source* for Social Security and Medicare?

Perhaps not coincidentally, Social Security is scheduled to deplete the combined trust fund reserves in 2033. The reserve depletion of Medicare is projected for 2030.[19]

Migrant Workers, Illegal Aliens, and Remittances

Are illegal aliens here to immigrate, or to work? The illegal aliens who overstayed their visas filed a statement of nonimmigrant intent before they entered the United States. So by definition these 4.4 million people are *migrants*. They have contractually agreed to temporarily reside in this country to

---

19. See Social Security and Medicare Boards of Trustees, Status of the Social Security and Medicare Programs, "A Summary of the 2014 Annual Reports," pages 1-5. Available at: www.ssa.gov/oact/trsum.

work, visit, and/or study for a specific time, and then they are legally required to *migrate* back to their country of origin before their visa expires.

The remainder of the 11 million-plus came here to work and earn money. Numerous studies reveal that illegal aliens are often "target wage earners," who come to the United States without intending to stay. They work until they meet their earnings target and then return home. To meet their earning targets, they often work long hours or double shifts, and/or have several jobs with multiple employers. This allows the "target wage earner" to not penalize the employer with overtime wages. The dream of someday enjoying the wealth that they have accumulated in the United States back in their country of origin is a common thread in their stories.

These "targeted earners" send billions of dollars home, mostly to Mexico. The money is sent to support immediate families and parents (who have no nationally sponsored retirement or health-care benefits), and sometimes some additional funds are sent for the construction of a future residence and to make other investments. Many of Mexico's citizens residing in the United States often live in poverty here in order to budget for weekly remittances to Mexico.

In 2009, the residents of Mexico received over $20 billion in transfer payments that originated in the United States of America.[20] The total annual remittances to Mexico and other Latin America countries may exceed $30 billion. These remittances are a source of foreign exchange that is as valuable as oil exports or tourism to their respective national economies.

Summary: The Real Truth

Who are the illegal aliens?

• They are by and large residents of Mexico and Central America.

• Our government has, in its databases for various agencies, the identities of a significant portion of those illegally residing in America.

---

20. "Migrants Remittances and Related Economic Flows," Congressional Budget Office, February 24, 2011, see exhibit 7. Available at: www.cbo.gov/publication/22012.

• Our government can also uncover almost as much information about illegal aliens as it can about U.S. citizens.

How did they get here?

• Surprisingly, 40% of the approximately 11 million illegal aliens, or 4.4 million, entered America on visitor, work, or student visas. They entered legally, with government permission and in possession of a passport issued by their country of origin. Most of the rest crossed our borders illegally.

How long have they been here?

• Over 85% of illegal alien adults have resided in the United States for over five years.

What do they do here?

• They work and earn a living!

• We have also learned that up to 75% of illegal aliens are, according to the IRS and the Social Security Administration, on employer payrolls and pay Social Security, Medicare, and other taxes on a regular pay period basis.

• That they are being paid "under the table" is more myth than fact.

What do they want here?

• The available data suggest that a significant portion of the illegal aliens are not interested in citizenship. Many (if not most) just want to come to the "land of opportunity," make some money, return home with their wealth, and resume their life in the country of their birth. *They are here for the work and nothing more.*

What's the real issue stopping reform?

• We learned that in 2007, Social Security and Medicare received almost $14 billion in funding from the earnings of illegal aliens. While the politicians in Washington publicly decry the illegal immigration problem, they have talked continually about this thing called "immigration reform." Privately they recognize that the federal budget benefits greatly from the presence of illegal aliens, who contribute 7.5% of their earnings while the employer matches that, for a total of 15% to Social Security and Medicare benefits, all of which illegal aliens are prohibited by federal law from receiving.

• We also learned that Mexico is an even a greater beneficiary than the U.S. government. Transfer payments, monies that were earned in the United States and sent to residents of Mexico, provided a $20 billion dollar-plus benefit to Mexico's economy. Additionally, those American dollars generally have far greater buying power in the economies of Mexico and other Central American countries (in some instances, a multiple of two or three times the buying power). Ask any American who has chosen to retire to one of the many "American enclaves" there. Many websites annually rank Mexico as one of the top 10 places to visit as a tourist because of its noteworthy affordability. Imagine how much further indigenous Mexican nationals can stretch those dollars coming from America!

Review

Let's take a moment and quickly review what we've covered in the first two chapters of this book:

Preface: Immigrants, Aliens, or Migrant Workers?

After reviewing the labels used in the media, the term "illegal alien" was chosen for this text because it most accurately describes the true nature and character of the individual in question and their legal status in America.

Chapter 1: The Dilemma (Quandary, Question, Problem ···)

A brief history of immigration showcased the wide range of immigration law enforcement that has been exercised in America since 1882. While some presidents have strictly enforced our immigration laws, most have not.

Chapter 2: Who Are the Illegal Aliens?

We brought into sharp focus the makeup of the alien population, how they got here, their work ethic, level of tax contribution, and their support of the family members they left behind.

In chapter 3 we are going to examine "The Employer's Tool Box."

What tools has the federal government provided the employer to ensure that the employers hire only legal workers?

And what if an employer unknowingly hires an illegal alien? How can they legally terminate them?

$\oint$

Chapter 3

The Employer's Tool Box

Given what we learned in chapter 2—that most illegal aliens are on employer payrolls and that the federal government knows who they are—shouldn't employers be able to tell who is legal and who isn't before they hire them? Aren't unscrupulous employers who knowingly hire illegal aliens part of the problem?

Let's look a little further at the tools created by the government for employers to use when hiring people. There are several: Form I-9, the E-Verify system, and the Social Security Number Verification System. Do these tools help employers determine who is and who isn't legal? Do they help protect employers from fines and penalties for knowingly hiring illegal aliens? This chapter will describe each of these tools and their limitations.

Form I-9

As a result of the passage of the Immigration Reform and Control Act of 1986, employers are required to complete U.S. Citizenship and Immigration Services Form I-9.[21] The purpose of this document is to verify the identity and employment authorization of each new employee (both citizen and noncitizen) hired after November 6, 1986.

The general instructions for Form I-9 state the following: "(1) the Employers may be fined if the form is not complete, (2) Employers are responsible for retaining completed forms, (3) The employer is not to mail the completed forms to the U.S. Citizenship and Immigration Services." (Why is it that the government [since September 6, 1986] does *not* want to verify this documentation or at least secure and retain this documentation in its data banks?)

The last page of the nine-page document provides a List of Acceptable Documents that may be used to complete the form. The acceptable documents are organized into three lists: A, B, and C. The employee may present one selection from list A, or one selection from list B and one selection

---

21. For more information on Form I-9, go to www.uscis.gov/i-9.

from list C. Most applicants choose the B&C list option; a driver's license/ID card and a Social Security account number card are chosen most often. The instructions state: "The employer must examine the employment eligibility and identity document(s) an employee presents to determine whether the document(s) appear to be genuine." [22] In this age of digital photography and Photoshop software, it is very difficult for the ordinary employer to determine if the provided documents appear genuine. Everyone knows world-class forgeries are readily available for a price.

Because the accurate completion and retention of the I-9 Form protects employers from fines and/or criminal prosecution (even if the provided documents are forgeries), employers overwhelmingly choose *not* to pay their employees (including illegal immigrants) under the table. This is why 75% of all illegal aliens are on regular payrolls.

E-Verify

In 1996, Congress passed the Illegal Immigration Reform and Immigrant Responsibility Act (IIRI-

---

22. Ibid.

RA), which required the Social Security Admin-istration (SSA) and U.S. Customs and Immigration Service (USCIS), formerly the Immigration and Naturalization Service, to conduct an employment verification pilot program. E-Verify is an Internet-based system that implements the requirements of IIRIRA by allowing U.S. employers to electronically verify the employment eligibility of their newly hired employees.[23] (Author's note: If you read the last sentence carefully, you will realize that the pro-gram does *not* allow an employer to use E-Verify to prescreen an applicant to determine if they are in the United States legally *before* they hire them). E-Verify is a voluntary program for most employers.

I encourage the reader to go online to the E-Verify portion of the U.S. Citizenship and Immigra-tion Services website, at www.uscis.gov/e-verify. Click on the "Publications" icon, then "Manuals and Guides," and choose "E-Verify User Manual."

The user manual is 84 pages in length. Pages 1 through 8 will provide you with a good summary of how the program works (or doesn't work?). It's an easy read. Page 8, or section 1.5, contains some

---

23. "E-Verify," U.S. Citizenship and Immigration Services website. Available at: www.uscis.gov/e-verify.

basic guidelines, titled "User Rules and Responsibilities." These guidelines list things that E-Verify users should and should not do. The "Must Do" list includes things any employer would do: ask for photo ID, collect SSN info, name, address, etc. But the items on the "Must Not Do" list (on p. 8 of the manual) are very important.

Here are the bullet points captured under the heading: "Employers participating in E-Verify MUST NOT":

• Use E-Verify to prescreen an applicant for employment.

• Create an E-Verify case for an employee who was hired before the employer signed the E-Verify MOU [memorandum of understanding].

• Take adverse action against an employee based on a case result unless E-Verify issues a Final Nonconfirmation.

• Terminate an employee during the E-Verify verification process, because he or she receives a TNC [Tentative Nonconfirmation].

> • Specify or request which Form I-9 documentation a newly hired employees must use.
>
> • *Use E-Verify to discriminate against ANY job applicant or new hire on the basis of his or her national origin, citizenship, or immigration status* [my emphasis].
>
> • Selectively verify the employment eligibility of a newly hired employee.
>
> • Share any user ID and/or password.

One of the most often stated causes of illegal immigration is that "employers *knowingly* hire illegal aliens." The E-Verify program is represented as a viable way of reducing the frequency with which employers hire illegal aliens. Yet the program requires the employer to first hire the employee based upon the presentation of certain documents that have yet to be determined to be genuine and valid. The employer is to complete the E-Verify process within the first three days of the new employee's tenure. If after submission the documents are suspected of being invalid (called Tentative Nonconfirmation, or TNC), the employer is *prohibited from firing* the individual. The goal of hiring only those employees who are in the United States legally has been sacrificed on the Altar of Political Correctness.

In many states, terminating an employee because their Form I-9 documents do not meet standards is grounds for a wrongful termination or a discrimination lawsuit. In some states, such as California, there are immigrant groups that specialize in legally pursuing this type of termination case.

The rest of the manual outlines the process by which the newly hired employee can contest a non-confirmation determination. The employer is required to provide the employee *in writing* with all the information necessary to contest a nonconfirmation determination. The employer must continue the individual's employment until such a time that the SSA and/or the Department of Homeland Security (DHS) renders a final determination of nonconfirmation (called a Final Nonconfirmation).

This process, as in any other government program, requires the *employee* to complete the necessary forms, meet related deadlines, and so on before a Final Nonconfirmation can be made. Please note that the employee in question is responsible for contacting SSA and/or DHS. If the employee's documents are forgeries, the employee will not be in a hurry to receive the Final Nonconfirmation, and they can do any number of things to slow down the process.

It appears that once an employer hires an illegal alien it is very difficult and possibly dangerous (business-wise) to fire that person. And it is *so very easy* for the employer to make a mistake! Further, it seems easy for the employee who is an illegal alien to slip through the cracks for an indeterminate length of time.

E-Verify is a voluntary program. Enrolling in the program requires an investment of time and is significantly complex. One of the many requirements of participation in the program is that the employer must display the poster titled "This Organization Participates in E-Verify." The poster must be displayed in both English and Spanish.

The poster states:

> Important: If the government cannot confirm that you are authorized to work, this employer is required to give you written instructions and an opportunity to contact DHS and/or the SSA, before taking adverse action against you, including terminating your employment.

Employers may not use E-Verify to prescreen job applicants and may not limit or influence the choice of documents you present to use for the Form I-9 [my emphasis].

The last paragraph asks the new hire/applicant the following: "If you believe that your employer has violated its responsibilities under this program, or has discriminated against you during the employment eligibility verification process based upon your national origin or citizenship status, please call the Office of Special Counsel," with telephone numbers of both DHS and the Justice Department. (Question: Whose interests are these government agencies acting in: the citizens of the United States? the government? the employer? or the employee—whose legal status is yet to be determined?)

The Notice portion of the poster, in the bottom right-hand corner, is the most telling: "Federal law requires all employers to verify the identity and employment eligibility of all persons hired to work in the United States." The problem is, employers have *no way* to independently verify the identity of applicants. They can only *record and report* the information that was provided by the applicants for the completion of Form I-9. The authenticity of those documents and the applicant's employment eligibility can be verified *only by the federal government.*

The government admits in the second paragraph that even they cannot always confirm an employee's eligibility. Yet the employer can safely terminate the employee only when E-Verify, via SSA and/or DHS, makes a final determination (Final Nonconfirmation) that the employee is not in the United States legally!

This program is represented to John Q. Public by the federal government, the politicians, and the media as an attempt to crack down on unscrupulous and predatory employers who knowingly hire illegal aliens. As you can see, the truth of the matter is, the employer has no way to determine before the employees are hired if they are in the United States legally. If an employer unintentionally (accidentally?) hires an individual for whom a Tentative Nonconfirmation is later rendered, they must continue to employ the person until such time that the federal government issues a Final Nonconfirmation. It is unclear how long it will take for that Final Nonconfirmation to be determined, if ever. In some unknown number of instances, employers are required to continue to employ individuals who on day three of their employment were determined by E-Verify as being tentatively nonconfirmed as illegal aliens. Employment is statutorily mandated to continue until some federal official at an unknown later date determines that the individual is recategorized with a Final Nonconfirmation and can no longer be lawfully employed.

I suspect that most Americans believe that the E-Verify Program intentionally gives employers the capability to prescreen, to clearly determine the legal status of applicants before they are hired. This would ensure that employers would not, or could not, hire illegal alien workers. But as you can see, any American who believes this to be true would be *wrong.*

Social Security Number Verification System (SSNVS)

This system offers to verify Social Security numbers for named individuals *after* an employer has already hired them. Like E-Verify, the Social Security Number Verification System (SSNVS) is a membership program. To become a member and use the system, an employer has to agree to the SSNVS Attestations, which begin as follows:

1. SSNVS should only be used for the purpose for which it is intended.

2. SSA will verify Social Security numbers (SSN's) solely to ensure the records of *current or former employees* [Author's note: You have to hire them first!] are correct for the purpose of completing the Internal Revenue Service (IRS) Form W-2 (Wage and Tax Statement).

3. It is illegal to use the service to verify SSN's of potential new hires or contractors or in the preparation of tax returns.[24]

There are 10 more bullet points in the list of SSNVS Attestations. Let me save you, the reader, the pain of reading them all and skip to the admonition, printed in boldface, at the end of the list. It reads: "If you rely on the information SSA provides regarding name and SSN verification to justify adverse action against a worker, you may violate State

---

24. Social Security Number Verification Service. SSA website. Available at: www.socialsecurity.gov/bso/services.htm.

or Federal law and be subject to legal consequences."[25] Clearly, using this system as a prescreening device is not legal. The risk for employers who use the system is that if they are ever investigated by this agency, it will not be difficult for the government to determine whether or not they used the system as a prescreening tool. Employers who have misused the system to avoid hiring illegal aliens are *guilty of a crime*. In the words of Lieutenant Commander Steve McGarrett, from the 1968 to 1980 version of *Hawaii Five-0*, "Book 'em, Danno."

Summary: The Real Truth

It's quite possible that this is not an exhaustive list. There may be other federal programs similar to these that I have missed. But my suspicion is that none of them will be any better at providing useful and beneficial information or guidance for employers wishing to avoid hiring illegal aliens.

The ineffectiveness of these "tools" has helped contribute to the stereotypical image of employers, projected by our politicians and the media, as people who go out of their way to *knowingly hire illegal*

---

25. Ibid.

aliens to operate their businesses. Here's a typical example: This is a question from a Gallup Poll conducted June 15-16 in 2013: "Would you vote for or against a law that would require U.S. business owners to check the immigration status of any employees they hire, with stiff fines and penalties for employers who knowingly hire unauthorized workers?" Seventy-seven percent of respondents were for such a law, 21% were against, and only 3% were unsure. Clearly people think employers need more policing.

Questions like these reinforce the public's incorrect preconceived notion that employers will not do the right thing unless they are threatened with stiff fines and penalties. Few people realize the truth: If an employer enrolls in the E-Verify Program, the employer is statutorily compelled to continue to employ a worker who is suspected of being an illegal immigrant until such a time that the E-Verify Program determines that the individual has received a Final Nonconfirmation. Only then can the employer lawfully (and safely) terminate the illegal alien worker.

Under our current system it is not possible for employers to know for a certainty if their new hires are legal or not.

The truth of the matter is that no employer wants to give the federal government *any reason* to single out their business for government scrutiny. Alleged violation of federal law is a serious matter. The need to prove that your business is innocent of any charges could easily damage the reputation and financial viability of your business. It could be economically fatal. Even if you win, you lose!

How easy would it be to use E-Verify as a pre-screening tool and hire only those job applicants who are approved by the program (i.e., by the government, who has knowledge of who is legal and who isn't)?

What would the status of illegal immigration be today if employers had tools that would easily enable them to hire only those individuals who are in the country legally in the first place?

Stiff fines and penalties for violations of law are already a fact of life for employers; what they need are tools to help them hire fully legal employees. Employees must be determined to be legal, by whatever means available, *before they are hired!*

At this point, you the reader should have an accurate understanding of the history of illegal immigration in America, an accurate profile of the illegal immigrants' tax-payer status (75% are tax payers), the length of illegal residents' stay (85% over 5 years), and the passport status of the illegal immigrants currently residing in America (40% hold passports). And you now can *easily* understand how so many business owners have come to employ those 11-plus million-plus illegal aliens.

You possess all the facts needed to easily understand *The Solution Whose Time Has Come.* Coming up next in chapter 4: The Proposal: The Authorized Guest Worker Program.

$\int$

Chapter 4

The Proposal: The Authorized Guest Worker Program

The immediate question for us is, how do we legitimize the presence of a large group of hardworking, law-abiding, contributing members to the common good, who entered the country illegally?

I have a simple solution: The Authorized Guest Worker Program. This program would provide a safe harbor for aliens who have entered the country illegally, are hard-working, do not have a criminal record, pay their taxes, have resided in the United States for at least two years, and are interested in joining a defined group that will enjoy the protection of the laws of the United States of America. They would be free from the fear of deportation for the 10-year life of the program.

Additionally, they would possess an Authorized Guest Worker identification card that would allow them lawful access to employment, provide a direct link to Authorized Guest Worker updates/ongoing requirements of membership, and initiate and secure a passport for the Guest Worker from their country of origin. Once the passport process is complete, the Authorized Guest Worker will enjoy legal and unimpeded travel across the U.S. border.

The goal of this program is to offer those individuals who are able to meet the program membership requirements and have entered the United States illegally a pathway to achieving a legal status that would allow them to remain in America.

It will not be a pathway to citizenship! The legal pathway to citizenship is well defined and has served America well for over 100 years. Membership in the program will specifically define, identify, and declare that the participant is not a U.S. citizen and is *not* being fast-tracked to citizenship.

Key Components of the Program

The Authorized Guest Worker Program will include the following components:

- Membership in the Authorized Guest Worker Program will be strictly voluntary.

• No new government bureaucracy will be created for the membership application process. The private sector will be used exclusively.

• All costs of the program will be paid by the Authorized Guest Worker applicant in the form of fees. The cost of the program will be self-liquidating.

• If the applicant for membership does not already possess a passport from their country of origin, the application for Authorized Guest Worker status will initiate the passport application process. This will ensure that the applicant will be compelled to register a name and identity that can be independently verified by their country of origin.

The passport-issuing countries will recognize the benefit of expediting the passport applications of those individuals seeking membership in the U.S. Authorized Guest Worker Program. Failure to do so would place at risk the approximately $30 billion a year in transfer payments that have historically been made by illegal aliens working in the United States to Mexico and other Central American countries. The net re-sult will be that all members of the Authorized Guest Worker Program will possess a valid passport from the country of their birth.

• At the completion of the application process, the illegal alien will be provided with an Author-ized Guest Worker Identification Card that will serve as a *passport to employment.* The Author-ized Guest Worker will be required to present this ID card to all prospective employers. The employer will in turn scan the card and receive a printed authorization to employ. This will ful-fill the employer Form I-9 requirement. The card will be scannable on any credit card read-er-enabled cash register. Additional card scanning capabilities will be developed.

• Guest Workers will be required to scan their ID cards whenever they cash their paychecks. The scanning of any card will trigger communi-cation between the worker and the federal government. That communication will be print-ed and provided in addition to the standard bank receipt to the guest worker. Those Au-thorized Guest Workers who do not receive a regular paycheck will still be required to scan their cards every two weeks. In addition to scanning the card at the bank, other methods will be developed (i.e., ATM terminals, Smart Phones, etc.).

• The program will have a one-year set-up period, followed by a two-year membership sign-up window, and a seven-year life (10-year sunset).

After the program is fully implemented and in operation for a reasonable period of time, it will be easier to understand what changes (if any) will need to be made before the expiration of the program. This will also allow illegal aliens (now Authorized Guest Workers) to make plans for their own future. Are they are going to remain in this country as a migrant worker, or start the naturalization process and become a United States citizen? Will they return home to their country of origin? The program will provide a 10-year window of opportunity to make those determinations.

We, the citizens of the United States of America, will need time to determine whether or not the program will be renewed, amended, or replaced. This 10-year period will allow all interested parties (including the Authorized Guest Workers) to offer for discussion and reasoned debate the possible extension or transformation of this program.

Perhaps with the successful implementation of this Authorized Guest Worker Program and the passage of time, *illegal immigration will become a distant memory.*

While many in the public eye campaign for immigration reform, others believe that our current immigration system has served the nation well. But the problem with our current immigration system is that it has not been able to quickly and accurately satisfy the fluctuating (sometimes large and uneven) demand for guest (migrant) workers.

Many individuals currently residing in the United States illegally would jump at the chance to come out of the shadows, achieve a recognized legal status, and live under the protection of U.S. laws. They would appreciate the opportunity to differentiate themselves from the other, less desirable illegal aliens. Their lawful participation in the Authorized Guest Worker Program would protect them from the threat of deportation.

This Authorized Guest Worker Program will satisfy the current and immediate demand for guest workers and will provide an opportunity for citizens of the United States of America to make an unhurried, thoughtful, and bipartisan determination about the future of the program.

Year One: Set-up Period

The registration process for the Guest Worker will be accomplished by a partnership effort involving private sector entrepreneurs, the credit card companies, and existing federal government agencies.

The registration process will exclusively utilize the Global Entry Kiosk used by the U.S. Customs Service's "Trusted Traveler Program" at U.S. airports that are identified as Customs Ports of Entry. Currently, the Global Entry Kiosk is used to prescreen individuals entering the United States. The device is a self-service unit that scans the individual's passport, asks a series of questions, digitally scans the individual's fingerprints, and takes a digital facial photograph. Upon completion of the process, the unit generates a receipt that is then taken to an actual customs agent for review and approval, whereupon the individual is granted entry into the country. You can see the Global Entry Kiosk in action on YouTube if you search for "Global

Entry PSA."[26] The Global Entry Kiosk, with some software enhancements and additional documentation, will essentially fulfill the very same role for the Authorized Guest Worker Program. The application process will collect the needed information, format it into a uniform package, and deliver it digitally to existing federal government agencies for further processing.

New software will need to be written to meet the needs of the Authorized Guest Worker application process and utilize the capabilities of the Global Entry Kiosk. Some additional peripheral devices will need to be added to expand the capability of the stock, off-the-shelf kiosk unit. Most notably, the program will need a document scanner for the paper application and a device to produce an Authorized Guest Worker identification card, complete with picture, unique new tax ID number, and a magnetic data strip, etc., much like a standard driver's license or bank card. The card would be delivered to the Authorized Guest Worker at the completion of the application process. These and

---

26. See U.S. Customs and Border Protection, *CBP Video: Global Entry PSA* (YouTube video). Available at: www.youtube.com/watch?v=EbbZWXIJKQ0.

other requirements will be determined by the needs of the application process.

Utilizing the "off-the-shelf, already been designed, tried, tested, and in use" Global Entry Kiosk makes the program's one-year set-up period readily achievable. The only alteration to the kiosk design that may be required is the capability to plug in the additional peripheral devices needed to complete the application process. Clearly, new units will need to be manufactured to meet the demand created by the application process. Any improvements that need to be made to the newly manufactured units must not significantly delay the manufacture of the kiosks or compromise the use of the units for their original purpose.

If the current manufacturers of the Global Entry Kiosk (such as Kiosk Information Systems) are unable to scale up production quickly enough to meet the demand, other manufacturers can be brought online. I'm sure that other manufacturers will be ready, willing, and able to meet the need. If you have any doubts, go to: www.kiosk.com and take a look at what they can do.

The cost of the Global Entry Kiosk, needed service, plus a $500 reassignment fee would be amortized for a two-year life. The cost of the kiosk, the reassignment fee, and the cost of any needed service during the sign-up period would be the responsibility of the kiosk operator. The unit would be used for the two-year sign-up window, and at the close of the membership period ownership of the kiosk would be transferred to the U.S. Customs and Immigration Service. The $500 reassignment fee would then be used by U.S. Customs and Immigration Service to repair, reprogram, refurbish, and redeploy the unit to a Port of Entry location to facilitate and improve the Port of Entry process. Thus as a direct result of this program the U.S. Customs and Immigration Service will be able to populate our ports of entry with additional Global Entry Kiosks to improve the timeliness, quality, and accuracy of the Port of Entry experience. *Border security would be measurably improved as a direct result of the Authorized Guest Worker Program.*

The recovery of these and related costs involved with these units will be achieved by the kiosk operator through the assessment of fees to be paid by those applying for Authorized Guest Worker status.

In summary, the Guest Worker application experience at the Global Entry Kiosk would include:

• Document scanning capability for the application

• Digital cameras for front, right, and left facial photographs

• Digital biometric scanner for a full, 10-fingerprint scan

• Digital video recording of the complete application process for inclusion into the applicant's record

• A digital video recording of the applicant taking the DNA cheek swab, complete with placement of the swab into the swab capsule. The device would require that the capsule be positioned so that the kiosk unit can digitally capture the bar code identification.

• A device to produce the Guest Worker identity card, with an ID picture, magnetic ID information strip, and a new unique taxpayer ID number (this number would replace previously misused SSA numbers).

• A credit card payment terminal. All payments will be made via a credit card, debit card, or prepaid debit card. This requirement will improve the safety of the application locations by eliminating the presence of cash. Proof of payment will be included in the applicant's record.

All of the digital data will be transmitted in real time via the credit card network to a secure federal facility for retention and future secure access. The DNA data and other information would follow via secured delivery by the U.S. Postal Service for digital inclusion into the applicant's data record.

Licensing requirements would need to be crafted for the kiosk operators collecting and processing the application data. At the very least, the individuals administering the application process must be U.S. citizens in possession of a current and valid U.S. passport. Additionally, they would have to pass the same background check administered to the authorized Guest Worker applicants.

The credit card companies would provide the secure communication conduit for the Authorized Guest Worker application and workplace hiring authorizations and would facilitate payday-linked Authorized Guest Worker communications.

Not only have the credit card companies en-rolled, communicated with, and received payments for tens of millions of credit card holders daily, they have established relationships and communication conduits with millions of retail locations. They have the infrastructure, expertise, and capacity to easily manage the communications needs and require-ments of this program.

To incentivize the participation, assistance, and support of the credit card companies, lawmakers will hasten to do what is necessary legislatively to allow credit card companies to include biometrics in the credit card authorization process. This will save the credit card industry hundreds of millions of dol-lars a year in fraudulent credit card charges. The savings would be applied to reducing credit card and bank charges for all Americans.

During the one-year set-up period, the media would publish information about the program and distribute it to those individuals who are interested in program membership. This set-up period would allow those individuals extra time to file delinquent tax returns and pay outstanding motor vehicle code fines, parking tickets, and the like, eliminating any and all potential barriers in advance that would delay or impede the membership process.

Years Two and Three: Membership Sign-up

Application for membership in the program will be open for only two years. Once the program is closed no further membership will be granted.

Some of the program membership requirements are as follows:

Proof of residence in the United States for the last two years

The wages of every illegal alien who has been paid through regular payrolls have been reported electronically to the Internal Revenue Service. The IRS will access its databases to internally determine that the claim of residence in the United States for the last two years by the program applicant is accurate. The Social Security numbers that the applicant has used in the past would be disclosed in the original application for membership in the program. The applicant will not have to produce any additional

W-2 documentation. The government already has this information in its databases.

Proof of payment of taxes for the last two years, payment of back taxes, or a signed agreement with the Internal Revenue Service to bring those taxes current

The same W-2 information would also be used to determine if the applicant has filed tax returns for the previous two years. If the applicant has paid the proper taxes, the applicant will not have to produce any documentation. If an applicant's tax payments are not current, proof of filing for back taxes would be required. At the very least, the applicant will need to enter into an agreement with the IRS to bring their taxes current.

Payment of a fine for illegally entering and residing in the United States

Potential Authorized Guest Workers may see having to pay a fine as a barrier to membership in the Authorized Guest Worker Program, reducing their already low pay. Small payroll deductions over a period of time could help ease the impact of the fine. While the payment of a fine is universally recognized as a consequence of breaking the law, it is important that this penalty is scaled to be reasonable and correct and not seen as a significant barrier to membership in this program.

A clean criminal background check

Successful completion of a criminal background check will dramatically improve the social, economic, and legal acceptance of the Authorized Guest Workers.

Demonstration of competence in conversational English by Year Four of the program

While some applicants would be able to demonstrate mastery of conversational English immediately, other applicants might be unable to do so. Moving this requirement to Year Four for all applicants will allow those who have not yet mastered English to have the time to do so. Failure to meet the requirement by the end of Year Four will disqualify the Authorized Guest Worker from continued participation in the program.

(Author's note: Every nation in the European Union [EU] requires demonstrated mastery of that nation's national language as a prerequisite to securing a guest worker visa. They believe that in order to work in their countries, you must speak, read, and understand the language of commerce.)

Private sector language training providers will be given the opportunity to develop online English language training programs to help applicants meet this requirement. The providers will create an approved online final exam that would utilize facial, voice recognition, and biometric software to certify that the Authorized Guest Worker has demonstrated mastery of conversational English and has met the standard. The provider would earn a fee, paid by the Guest Worker, for certifying that the competence standard has been met. All Authorized Guest Workers, even those who had mastery of English when they applied for the program, will be required to certify that the competency standard has been met before the year four deadline. A digital record of mastery of conversational English would be forwarded by the certification vendor for inclusion in the Guest Workers federal data record.

Disclosure of status when asked and ability to present the Authorized Guest Worker ID card at all times

In order to fully enjoy the benefits and full protection of U.S. laws, Authorized Guest Workers will need to openly demonstrate and declare their legal status in America to any and all members of civil authority, prospective employers, health care professionals, and the like. This will also allow Authorized Guest Workers to clearly and without confusion differentiate themselves from those who reside in the United States illegally.

Regular ID card swipe

Authorized Guest Workers will be required to swipe their ID card every payday (when they deposit their check at the bank) so the federal database can provide needed updates of any new requirements for the worker, etc. This communication document will be provided in addition to the standard deposit receipt.

Authorized Guest Workers will be able to swipe their ID card at any bank. The requirement will be that the Authorized Guest Worker must communicate with the federal government every two weeks, or a minimum of twice a month.

This would ensure that communication is maintained between the federal government and the Authorized Guest Worker in a timely manner. One of the many benefits of possessing an Authorized Guest Worker ID card is the ability to open and maintain a standard bank account. This will also make it easy for the bank to maintain that important communications link between their customers and the federal government. The bank would be required to provide this information in addition to a separate deposit receipt. The Authorized Guest Worker would thus have no legitimate reason to be ignorant of any changes, future requirements, or updates in their status.

Noncitizen status

Because Authorized Guest Workers are citizens of other countries, they are not eligible for any taxpayer-funded federal assistance programs, cannot vote, and cannot hold public office.

Once the public understands the special noncitizen status of the Authorized Guest Workers, they will begin to discard their old beliefs about illegal aliens. With time, they will accept the Authorized

Guest Worker as hard-working, law-abiding, contributing members to the common good who now reside in the United States legally.

Authorized Guest Workers recognize, understand, and accept the requirement to conduct themselves in a lawful manner. And they follow the laws of the United States of America. Further, Authorized Guest Workers fully understand and accept that the violation of U.S. law can result in suspension of Authorized Guest Worker status, resulting in deportation.

Membership in the Authorized Guest Worker program is like many other things in life: a goal requiring significant effort to achieve that can be destroyed in an instant.

Summary: The Real Truth

The Authorized Guest Worker Program will allow America to legitimize the presence of illegal aliens. It will allow those hard-working, taxpaying, background-checked individuals to become members of a defined special group, of which 85% have already lived illegally in this country for at least the last five years.

I suspect that by this point you may have experienced a whole range of emotions:

• **Anger** at your elected representatives for allowing, facilitating, and even encouraging the events that have delivered us to a time where our country is populated by 11-plus million illegal aliens.

• **Frustration** that there isn't leadership willing and able to craft a solution to end the exploitation of immigrant workers, the American economy, and federal / state / local government programs.

• **Disbelief** that things have gotten so far out of control when it can be so easily fixed!

It is my sincerest hope that this proposal will foster in the reader a genuine feeling of optimism.

The truth of the matter is: The Authorized Guest Worker Program is A Solution Whose Time Has Come.

$\oint$

Chapter 5

How Can the Private Sector Get This Done?

How will the Authorized Guest Worker Program be implemented?

You might imagine that a new government program would be required. But that's the beauty of this program. It's simple, it uses technology and information that's already in place, and it can harness the skills and innovation of American business. In fact, the program would depend on business rather than government to succeed.

As stated in chapter 4, "No new government bureaucracy will be created for the membership application process. The private sector will be used exclusively."

I don't want you to interpret the intention to conduct this activity in the private sector as a bias against the government. But in my opinion, the government is already fully engaged in the ongoing responsibilities of government and in the recent past has demonstrated that it is ill-suited to execute new, short-lived programs in a timely manner. Simply put: federal, state, and local bureaucracies operate best with programs that are well established and have existed for a significant period of time. The private sector is better suited to execute programs that have a defined beginning and a defined end. Business owners have experience and expertise in scaling up and scaling down operations (for example: construction projects, real estate development, civil engineering projects, etc.).

Private Sector Involvement in the Program

The program conception is simple and efficient. Still, preparing the system for the scale of the application process will be a huge undertaking. Because the membership window will be open for only two years, it will be particularly challenging to register

11-plus million people. To achieve this goal will take some "outside-the-box" entrepreneurial thinking, planning, and execution.

Education and technology

The application process itself will be very straightforward, as we have seen, but people will need to learn how it works. This program will generate a high level of interest, and as a result there will be a high public demand for the Authorized Guest Worker application information. Information about the application requirements and needed paperwork will be available to the general public through any number of public and private websites.

The process of educating the public would be similar to that at polling stations used in local elections. The polling stations are well organized and staffed by officials who assist the voters with the voting process. Voters are often coached and admonished in advance to bring their completed sample ballot with them so that their time in the voting booth will be minimized. Much of the same methodology would be used at the sites selected for the Authorized Guest Worker application process. Those organizations interested in providing Guest Worker application services, both profit and nonprofit, will develop websites that fully advertise, explain, and demonstrate their offered services, with full video presentations. Some enterprising individuals will probably make YouTube videos of the whole process to help people successfully complete the application process in record time.

Keep in mind that what the Authorized Guest Worker membership application process requires is simply gathering the needed data for submission to the federal government. This data (proof of residence, payment of taxes, criminal background checks, etc.) will all be verified off-site through the federal databases. Again, the application process is just a registration activity.

The Global Entry Kiosk is already designed as a self-service device. The addition of a document scanner, credit card terminal, and a device that can produce the Guest Worker ID card will require the assistance of the registration sites' employees. The applicant's paperwork would be prescreened to make sure that it is complete and to minimize the time spent at the kiosk. I estimate that completing an undocumented alien's application process in less than five minutes is readily achievable.

Cost

One of the items that we haven't discussed is the cost of registering for the program. Some hard costs will be easy to determine, and the federal government will have to develop a flat fee that will cover the government's cost of receiving, processing, formatting, and filing the Authorized Guest Worker applicant's data file. The federal government system will have to be designed to be easily accessed by other federal, state, and local authorized agencies pursuant to background checks or for individual searches for other needed documents.

The authorized licensed vendors providing Guest Worker application services would be free to set their own prices. Competition would determine the market price of these services, and Authorized Guest Worker applicants would be able to shop the market. Competition has demonstrated time and again that it delivers the best price to the customer.

Factors an Authorized Guest Worker Service startup might need to consider

Let's assume that 10 million people are interested in becoming Authorized Guest Workers. A two-year membership window would give us 730 days to register 10 million people, or 13,697 applicants a day on average.

Here's where the entrepreneurial, outside-the-box thinking is hard to anticipate. The individuals who are considering becoming licensed to provide application services for the undocumented aliens are going to look at the number of applicants and see dollar signs. Entrepreneurs will make their assumptions, build their models, gather their investors, and plunge into the opportunity. My belief is that this opportunity will provide a more than adequate capacity to meet the unknown demand.

Because of the potentially large number of Authorized Guest Worker applicants, selecting an entity / location or combination of entities / locations will be critical. The hours of operation, operating days of the week, and the number of kiosks available will be huge factors. More mundane considerations like accessibility, parking, easy vehicular access, ADA accessibility, restrooms, lighting, security, additional energy costs, public liability insurance, and the like will have to be considered.

The Entrepreneurs

So who are the entrepreneurs who might be interested in taking on this challenge?

Grass roots involvement

Ideal locations for application sites exist in every community in America. They are our nation's churches, Grange halls, service organization halls, and community centers. Although churches are not the only choice, they are possibly the best choice for a number of reasons. First of all, they are generally recognized as a place a person can go for assistance, protection, and refuge. Many of their members would embrace the registration and normalization of the undocumented alien population as a noble endeavor for the benefit of their fellow man.

Church locations are also well known in the community. Most have a distinctive architectural feature that is universally recognized: the church spire. Many have marquees that could easily be used to advertise the Authorized Guest Worker application kiosk's hours of operation. Many churches have non-sanctuary areas such as gyms, halls, or meeting areas that could be used for the registration equipment. As an alternative, others may consider the addition of a temporary modular building to house the Guest Worker registration activity.

Business involvement: The nuclear option

How about a major retailer with thousands of nationwide locations? Like WalMart? With over 4,100 locations spread across all 50 states, most open 24 hours a day, seven days a week, WalMart is an ideal location. Here's the raw math: on average each location would need to process only 7 applicants per day for the two-year period. Even if you limited the locations and reduced the number to 1,000 locations, on average each location would have to register only 28 applicants per day.

WalMart would have the flexibility and capability to move the kiosks from one location to another to meet the registration needs of the program. They already possess the scale, scope, and capability to meet even the currently unknown needs of a program like this.

Is it possible that the leaders of an organization like a WalMart would view this opportunity as their patriotic duty to their country, as well as a noble endeavor for the benefit of their fellow man? (Especially if they could make a profit in the process?)

It is inconceivable that, if given the opportunity, a WalMart or other national chain would be unable to successfully achieve the registration portion of the Authorized Guest Worker program within the two-year window. Who knows, they may even finish early!

The church option and the Walmart option represent the two extremes of a spectrum of options. I'm sure there is plenty of room between these two for other options, such as nonprofits or other service organizations.

Summary: The Real Truth

How will the Authorized Guest Worker Program be implemented?

• We have shown that no new government agencies or bureaucracies would need to be formed to handle the Authorized Guest Worker application forms and records.

• Existing Global Entry Kiosk designs can be easily modified and manufactured for this new purpose.

• Many entrepreneurial citizens will be clamoring for the opportunity to purchase and operate the kiosks.

• Locating the kiosks will be fairly easy, utilizing the private nonprofit sector (such as churches and service organizations), national chain stores, and small businesses.

The undocumented will embrace this program because they would benefit immediately. They would enjoy the many benefits of having an Authorized Guest Worker ID card, which would remove the historical barriers to their employment. And they would enjoy the protection of U.S. laws, free from worry about deportation. For many, the program might even be irresistible.

§

Chapter 6

The Long View

The immediate challenge for America is to legitimize the presence of a large group of hard-working, law-abiding, contributing members to the common good who entered the United States illegally from other countries. The goal of the Authorized Guest Worker Program is to offer those individuals who have entered the United States illegally a pathway to achieving a legal status that would allow them to remain at work in this country. Membership in the Authorized Guest Worker Program would require each participant in the program to secure a passport issued by their country of origin and pass a background check. The issuance of the passport would clearly define their noncitizen status.

Again, this program will *not* be a pathway to citizenship. The legal pathway to citizenship is separate and distinct from this program. The pathway to citizenship is accessible only through the U.S. Immigration and Naturalization Service. It is well defined and has been in operation for over 100 years. Participation in this program will not contribute to any preferential treatment in the immigration and naturalization process.

What About Nonparticipants?

Those who are unwilling or unable to meet the necessary requirements for becoming an Authorized Guest Worker will continue to "live in the shadows," and they will find it difficult to obtain employment after the membership deadline. An employers' clear first choice will be to employ only federally approved, lawful Authorized Guest Workers. To continue to employ unauthorized illegal aliens after the closure of the Authorized Guest Worker membership period will become very difficult, risky, and *illegal.*

Thus, at the end of the membership application period (the end of Year Three of the program) *the job magnet will be turned off.* Some of those who are unwilling or unable to qualify for the Authorized Guest Worker program will become discouraged and return home (self-deportation). Those who would not be able to qualify because they have a criminal record will be deported over time as a result of their inevitable contact with law enforcement, the Border Patrol, Homeland Security, USCIS, and other federal, state, and local agencies.

One of the primary benefits of the Authorized Guest Worker Program is that it allows the system to categorize illegal aliens into two groups: those who are able to pass a background check and those who are not. This differentiation will allow law enforcement agencies to narrow their focus and more easily identify individuals engaged in unlawful activities.

So what portion of the current 11-plus million undocumented aliens will become members of the Authorized Guest Worker Program? If the SSA estimate—that 75% of the illegal alien population receives a paycheck through normal payrolls—is accurate, the percentage of individuals who choose to become members of the Authorized Guest Worker Program and continue to live in the United States could be very large. Additionally, SSA data indicate that 85% of illegal aliens have been in the

United States for five years or more. Those two statistics combined would suggest that a large
percentage of the illegal alien population has lived
their lives here in a reasonably law-abiding manner.
They have not been arrested for unlawful activities,
incarcerated, and/or subject to deportation. They
have not run afoul of the law.

A Long-term Program?

As time passes, the number of Authorized Guest
Workers will inevitably decline. Some will age out of
the workforce (retire?), some will die, some may
even discover that the skills they have learned and
refined in America have a highly marketable value
in their country of origin and return home.

Many believe the estimated population of illegal
aliens peaked in 2009/2010. The Cable News Network, CNN, was one of many media sources that
reported this finding:

> The sharp decline began about five years ago,
> around the same time the U.S. housing market
> collapsed. Many construction jobs held by Mex-
> ican immigrants vanished. The continued
> weakness in the overall U.S. economy made it

harder to find other jobs as well. Although the great recession has officially ended, the job market is not back to what it was.

During the same years, U.S. officials have heightened enforcement of immigration laws along the border and elsewhere. Unauthorized border crossers have faced harsher penalties, and deportations have risen. We estimate that anywhere from 5% to 35% of the Mexicans who went home over the past five years did so involuntarily.

Another change in Mexico that is just beginning to affect migration streams is a deep decline in birth rates. In 1960, the fertility rate in Mexico was 7.3%, meaning, on average, a Mexican woman could expect to have seven children in her lifetime. By 2009, it had dropped to 2.4%. The declining birth rates have pushed up the median age of the Mexican population. This makes the age group in prime years of immigration (15- to 39-year-olds) a shrinking share of Mexico's population.

But even if Mexican immigration does begin to rise again, consider how far it has fallen. From 1995 through 2000, we estimate that 3 million Mexicans moved to the United States, and nearly 700,000, *including family members born in the United States*, went home. From 2005 through 2010, we estimate about 1.4 million Mexicans arrived, and the same number, including U.S.-born children, left. Considering everything, a return to the migration levels of the late 1990s now seems inconceivable.[27]

As positive changes in political, economic, and employment opportunities occur in Mexico and Central America, some aliens will decide to return home. For example, the Mexican government has decided to privatize portions of the government owned and operated petroleum industry, Pemex.[28,29] Pemex's crude oil production has de-

---

27. Jeffrey S. Passel and D'Vera Cohn, "Why Wave of Mexican Immigration Stopped," *CNN Opinion*, April 26, 2012.

28. "Mexican President Enrique Pena Nieto signed new energy laws [in August 2014] designed to transform a sector that has been dominated by the government for decades. Among the changes, private and foreign oil firms can compete with Pemex in exploration and production for the first time in 76 years, and a wholesale electricity market will provide competition to state power utility Commisión Federal de Electricidad." Lawrence Iliff, "Mexico's Pemex Adjusts Structure to Compete with Private Companies," *WSJ Business*, April 20, 2014.

clined by a third over the last decade. (Author's note: Pemex funds about one-third of Mexico's federal budget.) The Mexican government is betting that by allowing the private sector to participate in Mexico's oil production, they can significantly reverse the decline. Many Mexican nationals working in American oilfields would see this as an irresistible opportunity to return home. A circumstance like this and others could cause the population of Authorized Guest Workers to decline further.

As the population of Authorized Guest Workers naturally declines, a system will be needed to replenish the demand for Authorized Guest Workers. Probably the easiest solution would be to expand the guest worker visa program with a new category. How about a migrant worker visa? This would allow us to return to the practice of matching national needs with the number of migrant worker visas issued.

---

29. "Pemex's crude-oil production peaked in 2004 at about 3.4 million barrels a day, according to company figures. The fields were declining, then suddenly they stopped declining and production stayed at 2.5 million barrels a day. Lawrence Iliff, "Mexico's Pemex Lowers Expected Oil Output for 2014," *WSJ Business,* April 22, 2014.

Is it possible that in a few short years this country could become a place where illegal immigration becomes a distant bad memory?

Can It Really Be This Simple?

All we have to do is allow illegal aliens who can qualify for the program to step out of the shadows—legally declare who they are—and provide them with a way to prove their good character (i.e., background check, payment of taxes, etc.) in exchange for a legal noncitizen status that provides them with the benefits and protection of U.S. laws, freedom of travel, and the acceptance of the American public.

Adoption of this simple concept would allow Americans and Authorized Guest Workers alike to look forward to a future where life is less stressful and more predictable and normal.

Rather than focusing on each other, together we could focus on building a better future.

Many may be critical of this work. They will find it difficult to set aside their political bias / point of view and evaluate this program in the light of day, based on the facts, data, and merit of the arguments. They will say something to the effect that it is incomplete, or that the program is just too simplistic. To some degree they may be correct. Let's take a look.

Incomplete?

The Authorized Guest Worker Program presents a framework that provides the basic structure, allowing for the private sector to fill in the blanks. No one individual can possess all the technical, operational, and management expertise needed to ensure the success of the program. The private sector can and will meet the challenge and create what (every) government is ill-equipped to produce and execute. The private sector will fill in the blanks.

The private sector is in the middle of a digital revolution: smart phones, iPhones, social media, apps, etc. Can you imagine what technological breakthroughs the private sector will create to produce a seamless, vibrant, and easily executed Authorized Guest Worker Program? The innovation that has created Facebook, Twitter, and Amazon can more than fill in the blanks. All we have to do is define the program, provide the structure, identify the participating government agencies, and then get the hell out of the way.

It's incomplete by design!

Too simple?

Some might argue that the immigration issue is just too complex to be tackled by one program. And they're right. This program is not a panacea; it has a single intent: Its core concept is to give all illegal aliens the opportunity to become lawful members of an exclusive group, people who can demonstrate that they are hard-working, law-abiding, taxpaying, and honorable individuals. They will be given the opportunity to clearly and legally differentiate themselves from those individuals whose presence in this or any country would not be desirable.

Membership in the program will provide the Authorized Guest Worker with an ID card that provides legal access to a job, and when used in conjunction with their passport, the *freedom to travel home*. Many illegal aliens have been trapped in the United States and have not been able to visit family members outside the United States for years. This program would allow them the opportunity to be reunited with their families, friends, and relatives. *They can resume a normal life.*

The adoption of the Authorized Guest Worker Program would produce a beneficial ripple effect throughout the nation. Members of the program would clearly recognize that failure to follow the requirements of the program (paying their taxes, staying out of trouble with the law, etc.) will result in deportation. With the federal government possessing all of their passport information, taxpayer information, fingerprints, DNA, and so on, workers would be inspired to tread the straight and narrow and conduct their lives in a lawful manner.

It's simple by design!

Ripple Effects

The program is simple, but its effects would be felt in multiple sectors: law enforcement, labor, fiscal policy, road safety, and border security.

Law enforcement

As stated earlier, this program would allow law enforcement at all levels to focus its attention on the *unauthorized* portion of the alien population. With the passage of time, those who have not passed the background check will be discovered and deported, further reducing the population of those individuals who reside in the in the United States illegally.

Wages

An unknown number of currently illegal aliens will not be able to qualify for membership in the Authorized Guest Worker program. These individuals will find it very difficult to find employment after the membership deadline. For this reason, some will self-deport, and the remainder will be deported as they come into contact with government and law enforcement officials. As these individuals leave the country, their abandoned jobs will be absorbed by legal workers. These circumstances will contribute to a reduction in unemployment. Some economists may even suggest that the replacement of an unknown number of low-pay and low-skill illegal aliens with legal workers will stimulate an increase in wages.

Tax revenue

It's highly probable that revenues to the U.S. Treasury will increase. As many individuals qualify for the Authorized Guest Worker program, they will recognize that filing factual, accurate, and honest income tax returns will ensure their continued participation in the program, because the consequence for not doing so could lead to deportation. (And, on

the other hand, the benefits of the program are
many and varied.)

Car insurance

Some of the beneficial ripple effects of this program
are not readily apparent but will be potentially
hugely beneficial to society at large. While illegal
aliens cannot currently avoid many socially beneficial taxes and other payments such as sales taxes
and property taxes (even as a renter, a portion of
the rent paid to one's landlord contributes to property taxes), many do not consider automobile
liability insurance necessary, even though it is statutorily required in most states. The four border
states of California, Arizona, New Mexico, and Texas have an uninsured motorist rate of 12% to 26%:
California at 15%; Arizona, 12%; New Mexico,
26%; and Texas, 15%.[30] In order to maintain their
membership in the Authorized Guest Worker Program, the Guest Workers will need to comply with
the law by buying and keeping up their automobile
insurance, thus reducing the percentage of uninsured motorists in those states to the average level

---

30. "How Many Drivers Don't Have Auto Insurance?" AutoInsurance.org website. Available at: www.autoinsurance.org/how-many-drivers-dont-have-auto-
insurance/.

of other states, which would reduce the rates for all insured motorists.

Border security

While enhancing border security is not a design element of the program, once the Authorized Guest Worker membership application period comes to an end (at the close of Year Three) the opportunity for illegal aliens to find jobs in the United States will be dramatically reduced. The ability of *nonauthorized* guest workers to secure employment here will significantly decline: the end of the application period may even eliminate the flow of illegal aliens crossing our borders because the jobs for illegal aliens will be gone. This reduction will allow Border Patrol to concentrate more fully on other criminal activities.

This is a 10-year program with a sunset clause (it ends 10 years after it begins, unless renewed by Congress), giving our country much needed breathing room to determine a new immigration / migration policy for the future. Those 10 years will allow plenty of time to absorb the public's input, time to test alternatives to our current policy, and time to just plain get it right!

This is not an exhaustive list of the "ripple effect" benefits. The bottom line: The Authorized Guest Worker Program will, over time, draw all of the program participants into the economic, religious, and societal mainstream of American life.

In Summary: The Real Truth

The Authorized Guest Worker Program will allow that portion of the illegal alien population that can meet the program requirements to remain in the United States for the duration of the program. These are the individuals who have demonstrated their lawful contribution to the common good. They are worthy of our trust for inclusion into this mutually beneficial program. They have earned this opportunity and our help.

What about the others? Many of them would not be welcome even in their own countries. Why would we want to allow these individuals to remain here and continue to victimize our citizens, government programs, and the legitimate members of the Authorized Guest Worker Program?

We are under no obligation to continue to house these undesirable individuals in the United States of America. They need to go home *now*.

The United States of America is our home, and like all homeowners we have the *right* to know just exactly who is a guest (worker) in our home!

ƒ

Afterword

Now What?

You now know:

1. The dictionary definitions for "immigrants," "aliens," and "migrant workers"

2. A brief history of illegal immigration in America

3. Who the illegal aliens are

4. The tools available to employers to ensure that they only hire legal workers

5. The key components of the Authorized Guest Worker Program

6. How the private sector can complete the registration process within the two-year window

7. How the implementation of this program will benefit America, benefit Authorized Guest Workers, and end illegal immigration as we know it

The Authorized Guest Worker program is The Solution Whose Time Has Come. Now that you have the burden of truth, what are you going to do with it?

What can you do? You are only one person! How can individual Americans like you and me share the truth and elevate the concept of the Authorized Guest Worker Program to the national level?

How Can We Do This?

Mainstream America is ready for a change. Comprehensive Immigration Reform (CIR) is back on the front page. Like it or not, politicians with their votes are going to determine the way forward for America. So to effect change we must start with the politicians.

Many politicians are trapped by the mistaken belief that illegal aliens, who are bona fide citizens of another country, are interested in abandoning their culture, their history, and their identity to be allowed to continue to live and earn money in the United States. They believe that all illegal aliens are more than willing to abandon their birthrights, culture, and history to become Americans. The politicians' belief is that these newly minted citizens will show their appreciation by forever voting for the political party that provided them with the gift of citizenship and unencumbered access to federal, state, and local benefits/programs.

(Author's note: This is an example of how politicians "monetize" their actions by providing material goods or special benefits for some voters, and in this case *imaginary* future voters.)

I suspect that many of our politicians are so invested in the minutia of Comprehensive Immigration Reform that they just haven't had the time to think of any other solution. We may be surprised how quickly some of our elected representatives embrace this new concept once they are exposed to the idea of the Authorized Guest Worker Program.

So, let's present them with this idea. This book, *The Immigration Solution*, is your handbook for making change happen. The Summary sections at the end of the chapters provided you with a healthy supply of talking points: take these to your neighbors, your friends, and most importantly, your elected officials. Email all of your congressional representatives, even the ones you disagree with. Call them (phone calls count more than emails). Please don't underestimate the power of your clear, concise, nonpartisan, fact-filled, well-reasoned message. And please resist the urge to "emote." Don't scold them, *educate them.*

Contacts

- **Senate:**
www.senate.gov/senators/contact/.
Choose a state or choose a senator.

- **House of Representatives:**
www.house.gov/representatives/. Choose a state or choose a representative.

As you've witnessed in this book, I've used the Internet extensively to gather facts (truth) for this book. You, too, can easily use the Internet to multiply your "only one person status" by emailing all of your congressional representatives.

We Can Do This!

So now that you are exposing your elected representatives to the Immigration Solution, who's next? Everyone else!

The Internet is playing a huge, ever-increasing role in political messaging, outreach, and coordination. It has already been instrumental in bringing together thousands of people in largely leaderless grassroots movements organized around central themes. Most Americans came to these movements *on their own.* They didn't have to be persuaded by the media, politicians, or political parties.

The movements began from a grassroots level: regular people communicating with one another over the Internet via emails, blogs, networking, social media, Facebook, Twitter, websites, and so on. As this movement grew, talk radio and cable television became part of the mix. Predictably, some natural leaders emerged. Meetings were scheduled and events were planned—and change came. This is probably old news for most of you. I suspect many of you participated in these movements.

How can you get the concept of the Authorized Guest Worker Program into a position to not only make the front page of newspapers, but to also be a major topic of discussion on talk radio, cable news, YouTube, and the Internet? Re-read the above: You can do this!

All the methods, strategies, techniques, and human resources used in the past are available to you today. They still exist. Nothing needs to be invented, designed, or created.

I, You, We, already have all we need to start the conversations that will lead to a grassroots movement that gets the Authorized Guest Worker Program into the national dialogue.

You've got your handbook. Share the information, share the book, and inspire others to get the Authorized Guest Worker Program going!

The Immigration Solution is an idea
whose time has come.
You can, we can, our country can
end illegal immigration in three years!
Stand up and make it happen!

$

Acknowledgments

This has been a long and difficult process. I sometimes thought I wouldn't get through it, but for the help of a few very special people:

Thanks to my parents for being Americans and teaching me to value my home and country. Thanks to our Founders for creating the Greatest Nation in the world. Thanks to my readers; we can continue on the legacy of our Founders if we try.

Thanks to Patricia for your inspiration and supreme editing skills. Thank you, Alan. We could not have imagined a better book cover–you have truly outdone yourself. Thank you, Sharon—you have been a friend and inspiration throughout the many years our families have been acquainted. And special thanks to my children; they put up with me and push me forward, they offer me a sounding board, and they are wonderful people I am fortunate to know. And special thanks to my wife. She does it all—plus she types much faster than I do, and she knows how to turn a phrase.

I am truly a lucky man!

www.ingramcontent.com/pod-product-compliance
Lightning Source LLC
Chambersburg PA
CBHW070809280326
41934CB00012B/3127